I Don't Wanna Sleep

I Don't Wanna Sleep

Written by Jerry Ariza

Illustrated by Lucy Shin

For Mika, Molly, & Emmett

Nothing in this life
has brought me more joy
than being yours.

Papa, I don't wanna sleep,
I don't like it.

I dont like the dark,
and I don't like the quiet.

Let's sleep, and we'll wake up
to the bright morning sun.

Just rest and I'll hold you
until your dreams come.

Papa, I don't wanna sleep,
let's stay awake.

I don't wanna dream,
my dreams might be strange.

Dreams are just pictures
you paint in your mind.

You can make them your way.
If you want, you can fly!

Good night, baby girl.
Sleep tight now and know,

That with every gentle moonbeam
my love for you grows.

So with every new sunrise
at the end of the night,

Be grateful for life,
safe and warm in the light.

I don't wanna brush!
I don't wanna relax!

Mama, I'm hungry.
I wanna eat snacks.

We brush every day
to have clean and strong teeth.

Now, it's time for your bed,
not for food. It's time to sleep.

But Mama, I'm not sleepy.
I wanna stay awake.

I wanna read books,
and I still wanna play.

Sleep now, and we'll wake
to the warmth of the morning,

A new day for writing
an amazing new story.

Goodnight, baby boy.
As you drift into slumber,

I want you to know,
and to always remember,

That my love will follow,
wherever you go.

No matter the distance,
however you grow.

I watch you each day,
as you play and you grow.

ようこそ日本へ！

And I pray for your safety,
wherever you go.

I hope that your future
is sunny and bright.

And that happiness finds you
as you bring the world light.

Sweet Dreams

www.ingramcontent.com/pod-product-compliance
Lightning Source LLC
Chambersburg PA
CBHW042024090426
42811CB00016B/1737